THOMAS EDISON

A Brilliant Inventor

By the Editors of TIME FOR KIDS
WITH LISA deMAURO

HarperCollinsPublishers

About the Author: Lisa deMauro is the author of several books and magazine articles for young people. She lives in Westchester County, New York, with her husband and two children. The author has spent many happy hours in Menlo Park, New Jersey, where Thomas Edison once lived.

Library of Congress Cataloging-in-Publication Data is available.
ISBN 0-06-057611-1 (pbk). — ISBN 0-06-057612-X (trade)

1 2 3 4 5 6 7 8 9 10
First Edition

Photography and Illustration Credits:
Cover: U.S. Department of the Interior, NPS, Edison National Historic Site; inside cover flap: Bettmann/Corbis; title page: The Granger Collection, NY; table of contents: Hulton Archive/Getty Images; facing p.1: Hulton Archive/Getty Images; p.1: Walter Sanders/Time Life Pictures/Getty Images; p.2: U.S. Department of the Interior, NPS, Edison National Historic Site; p.3: Corbis; p.4: U.S. Department of the Interior, NPS, Edison National Historic Site; p.5 top: U.S. Department of the Interior, NPS, Edison National Historic Site; p.5 bottom: The Granger Collection, NY; p.6: Layne Kennedy/Corbis; p.7: Corbis; p.8 top: Hulton Archive/Getty Images; p.8 bottom: The Granger Collection, NY; p.9 top: Mansell/Time Life Pictures/Getty Images; p.10: The Granger Collection, NY; p.11: The Granger Collection, NY; p.12: U.S. Department of the Interior, NPS, Edison National Historic Site; p.13: The Granger Collection, NY; p.14 top: North Wind Picture Archive; p.15: North Wind Picture Archive; p.16 top: The Granger Collection, NY; p.16 bottom: C. Borland/Photolink/Photodisc; p.17: Corbis; p.18: The Granger Collection, NY; p.19: North Wind Picture Archive; p.20: http://www.uspto.gov/patft/index.htm; P.21: North Wind Picture Archive; p.22: U.S. Department of the Interior, NPS, Edison National Historic Site; p.23 left: U.S. Department of the Interior, NPS, Edison National Historic Site; p.23 right: Bettmann/Corbis; p.24: The Granger Collection, NY; p.25 top: North Wind Picture Archive; p.25 bottom: Hulton Archive/Getty Images; p.26 top: The Granger Collection, NY; p.26 bottom: The Granger Collection, NY; p.27 top: The Granger Collection, NY; p.27 bottom: Lynn Goldsmith/Corbis; p.29: courtesy Illustration House; p.30 right: U.S. Department of the Interior, NPS, Edison National Historic Site; p.31: Bettmann/Corbis; p.32: Hulton Archive/Getty Images; p.33: U.S. Department of the Interior, NPS, Edison National Historic Site; p.34: Bettmann/Corbis; p.36: Hulton Archive/Getty Images; p.37 top: Bettmann/Corbis; p.37 bottom: The Granger Collection, NY; p.39 top: The Granger Collection, NY; p.39 bottom: U.S. Department of the Interior, NPS, Edison National Historic Site; p.40 top: U.S. Department of the Interior, NPS, Edison National Historic Site; p.40 bottom: Corbis; p.41: The Granger Collection, NY; p.44 #1: U.S. Department of the Interior, NPS, Edison National Historic Site; p.43 top: Alain Nogues/Corbis Sygma; p.43 bottom: C.Squared Studios/Photodisc; p.44 #1: Hulton Archive/Getty Images; p.44 #2: North Wind Picture Archive; p.44 #3: Foodpix/Rita Maas; p.44 #4: Underwood & Underwood/Corbis; back cover: The Granger Collection, NY

Acknowledgments:
For TIME FOR KIDS: Editorial Director: Keith Garton; Editor: Jonathan Rosenbloom; Art Director: Rachel Smith; Designer: Esta Shapiro; Photography Editor: Bettina Stamen/Jacqui Wong

 Find out more at www.timeforkids.com/bio/edison

CONTENTS

►STANDING TALL
Thomas Edison poses in his
Menlo Park lab filled with
beakers and test tubes.

CHAPTER 1

Let There Be

LIGHT

It was New Year's Eve, 1879. An inventor named Thomas Alva Edison was about to do something that had never been done before. On that December night, he was going to introduce the world to a new kind of light.

In Edison's time, people used lamps filled with oil or gas to see in the dark. But these lights could start fires easily. Some of them gave off sooty smoke or bad smells. Many needed to

▲ EARLY LIGHTING
This was an early
American oil lamp.

1

be refilled often. And they only lit up a small area.

For years, inventors had tried to make lightbulbs, but all their bulbs had problems. Some were so bright that they hurt people's eyes. Others were too expensive for people to use at home. And most burned out too quickly—almost as soon as they were turned on!

▲ WATTS NEW?
This is a model of Edison's first successful lightbulb.

No one had been able to make a lightbulb that was *practical*. Most people believed it could never be done. But Thomas Edison thought it could. After months of failure, he said he *had* made such a bulb! And he would prove it that very night!

Edison's workshop was in Menlo Park, New Jersey. It was a sleepy little village with a few houses, stores, and a train station. Edison set up many of his lightbulbs in his shop. He put lights in the houses and in the train station. He put some of his lights on poles that dotted the town's paths. All the electric lights were connected to one switch. When the switch was turned on, Menlo Park would light up all at once!

▶ EDISON'S HOUSE was in Menlo Park, New Jersey, the site of the first "electric village."

When people heard about Edison's "electric village," they were curious. Was it possible? They wanted to see for themselves. That New Year's Eve about three thousand people headed for Menlo Park. The railroad company had to add more trains just to carry all the sightseers!

The visitors were amazed to see the little New Jersey town glowing with warm, yellow light. It was like magic. The lights didn't cast gloomy shadows or hurt the eyes. They made the town look like something from a dream.

But it wasn't a dream. It was the dawn of a new age.

"Genius is one percent inspiration, ninety-nine percent perspiration."

—THOMAS EDISON

I. A. EDISON.
Electric-Lights.
No. 214,636. Patented April 22, 1879.

ted Mar. 1, 1887.

CHAPTER 2

Little Al's

BOYHOOD

homas Edison's story begins with his parents, Samuel and Nancy. The couple was married in 1828. Samuel Edison couldn't read or write very well, but he had lots of big ideas. He tried many ways of making a living. He worked as a sailor, a carpenter, and a tailor. Nancy Edison was educated, which was unusual for women in those days. She had even taught school as a teen. Nancy was also very religious.

▲ **NANCY EDISON taught school when she was a teenager.**

Samuel and Nancy had six children together, but the three youngest had died.

Then on February 11, 1847, the couple had another baby. Thomas Alva Edison was born in Milan, Ohio. The family called him "Little Al."

Little Al Edison was always getting into trouble. When he was two, he wanted to see if he could hatch goose eggs. He knew that the mother goose sat on her eggs to hatch them. So Al sat on the eggs himself. That was the end of the eggs!

When he was a little older, Al was

▲ LITTLE AL was always getting into trouble. As a child, he was often sick.

5

▲ **THIS IS THE HOUSE** in Milan, Ohio, where Al was born. Today it is a museum where visitors can see some of his early inventions and learn more about the Edison family.

curious about how birds flew. He knew that birds ate worms. He guessed that eating worms might be the answer. Al mashed up some worms and water. Then he talked a very trusting friend into drinking the mixture. That made her pretty sick. (It *didn't* make her fly!) And Al was in trouble again.

Al wasn't looking for trouble. Since he was naturally curious, he was always looking for answers. He was just trying to understand why things worked the way they did—and how things could be made to work better.

Trouble at School

When Al was seven, the Edisons moved to Port Huron, Michigan. Al started going to a one-room school there, but he had problems. He didn't like to sit still. He didn't want to work on his lessons. He was often daydreaming when the teacher called on him. If Al asked too many questions, the teacher got angry.

Al was also losing his hearing. Sometimes he may not have heard the teacher asking him a question. This made the teacher more upset.

After only three months, the teacher said that Al didn't belong in school. He said Al's brain didn't work right. Al was very upset and hurt. He went home and told his mother what had happened.

Nancy Edison got very angry! She took Al right back to

▲ AS A CHILD, Al began to lose his hearing. This picture was taken when Al was about seven.

I. A. EDISON.
Electric-Lights.
No. 214,636. Patented April 22, 1879.
...ted Mar. 1, 1887.

Fig.2.

school. Nancy told the teacher that he was wrong. Al was even smarter than the teacher, she said. Then she took her son home. That was the end of classroom learning for young Al.

Learning from Books

▲ LITTLE AL read books like this when he was a small child.

Nancy Edison taught Al at home. She and Samuel were happy to try to answer all of Al's questions. In fact, they liked it when Al asked questions and they encouraged him to do so.

When Nancy taught Al to read, new worlds opened up to him. He read as much as he could. He liked English literature, especially the plays and poems by William Shakespeare. Al loved to read books about history and science. The science books fascinated him. They gave him the idea to do experiments. They also taught

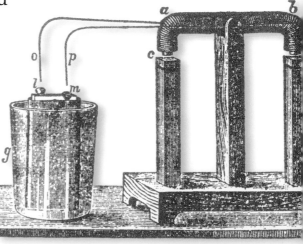

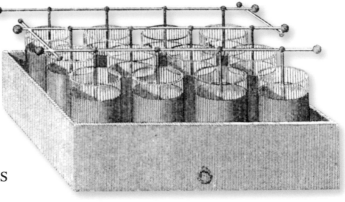

him about something that would change his life—electricity.

Electricity is a part of nature. (For example, think about lightning bolts!) Electricity had always been around, but no one knew how to make it or what to do with it. In the 1600s scientists began to take the first steps in figuring out how to *make* electricity.

By the 1840s scientists knew how to make a battery and an electric motor. People were just starting to find ways to *use* electricity. But that was just the beginning. Electricity was like a new land, waiting to be explored. And anyone with a curious mind could go exploring. Al loved the idea of coming up with new ideas. He didn't realize it at the time, but his curious mind and his love of asking questions would lead him to change the world.

◀ EARLY ELECTRIC MOTORS were being developed in the middle of the 1800s.

CHAPTER 3

The Amazing
TELEGRAPH

I n the 1800s people began traveling more quickly in the United States—by railroad. More and more track was being laid each week, connecting faraway places.

When Al was twelve years old, he got a job selling goods on board a train. (In the 1800s many children worked instead of going to school.) Al took the Port Huron train every morning to Detroit. During the three-hour trip, he walked up and down the aisle, selling fruits and sandwiches. When he got to Detroit, Al had hours

▲ READ ALL ABOUT IT! Al sold newspapers, candy, and fruit on the train.

to fill before the train left again. He used the time to buy newspapers, food, candy, books, and postcards, which he sold on the trip home.

Al had a lot of spare time during the train rides. So he decided to do science experiments. He never liked to waste a second! Al bought chemicals during his stopover time in Detroit. He asked the conductor to let

◄ TRAIN rides in Al's time were very bumpy.

him set up a little lab in the baggage car. After selling his goods, he went back to his lab. One day there was an accident. As the train lurched along, a chemical in Al's lab fell to the floor and caused a fire in the baggage car! The train crew put the fire out before it caused much damage. Luckily no one was hurt. But that was the end of Al's rolling lab.

News on Wheels

Al didn't give up. He had another big idea. Something that would keep him busy *and* make money! He could print a newspaper on the train! Al got a small printing press from a newspaper in Detroit. Then he wrote stories that he thought his customers would want to read.

Al wrote about local news and about the railroad workers. He included train

▶ WHEN HE was fourteen, Al was already on the road to success.

schedules and jokes. Then he printed *The Weekly Herald* in the baggage car. Hundreds of passengers bought Al's little paper.

For his whole life, Al would use his imagination to look at things in a new way. He would come up with ideas for items that he thought people might want. And then he would work hard—very hard—to turn his ideas into something real.

For the next few years, Al continued to work on the railroad. But he didn't continue to be called "Al." By the time he was fifteen, he felt he had outgrown his baby name. Now he wanted people to call him "Tom."

Tom had a good job working on the train. But he was much more interested in the telegraph.

Samuel F. B. Morse had invented the telegraph a few years before Tom was born. Using this machine, a person could

▲ SAMUEL MORSE INVENTED the telegraph in 1840.

send coded messages over a wire to someone far away. Before the telegraph,

Morse CODE

Morse created a special alphabet that was used to send messages over the telegraph. The code was made up of short clicks ("dots") and long clicks ("dashes"). The dots and dashes stood for the letters of the alphabet. A person could spell words with Morse code and send the message by telegraph wire to a distant place. Try writing your name in Morse code.

▲ **TAP DANCING FINGERS!**
The clicker was used to send messages in Morse code.

A .-	N -.
B -...	O ---
C -.-.	P .--.
D -..	Q --.-
E .	R .-.
F ..-.	S ...
G --.	T -
H	U ..-
I ..	V ...-
J .---	W .--
K -.-	X -..-
L .-..	Y -.--
M --	Z --..

a message could travel only as fast as it could be carried. Mail was carried by foot, by horse, by boat, or by train. Now messages could race across the miles in an instant!

The telegraph was a great help to the railroad companies. For the first time, news of schedule changes could be sent ahead of the train. Weather problems and accidents could be reported up and down the line. The telegraph made railroad travel safer. And the railroads made more jobs for telegraphers.

Tom liked to watch the telegrapher do his work. One day he got an idea. He could use the telegraph to advertise!

Tom knew that people were eager to get the latest news of the Civil War. (This bloody war raged between the northern and southern states in the early 1860s.)

On April 6, 1862, there was a very big battle in Shiloh, Tennessee. If Tom could let people know that he had news of the battle, he would sell a lot of newspapers. (These were not his own little papers. He bought these from the newspaper office in Detroit.) Tom

▶ TELEGRAPH POLES were put up all along the tracks.

T. A. EDISON.
Electric-Lights.
No. 214,636. Patented April 22, 1879.

ated Mar. 1, 1887.

Fig. 2.

◀ PEOPLE gathered at railroad stations to travel—and to read the latest news!

asked the railroad telegrapher to send a message with news of the battle to all the stations along the line. The headlines were written on chalkboards at the

Building a
RAILROAD

In 1861 it took months to travel from the East Coast to the West Coast. People went around South America by ship or overland by wagon, stagecoach, or on foot.

▲ STAGECOACHES were one way to travel cross-country.

A train trip across the United States would be much shorter. So in 1862 President Abraham Lincoln signed the Pacific Railroad Act. Two companies—the Union Pacific and the Central Pacific—began to build the railroad. The Union Pacific would start in Omaha, Nebraska, and build westward. The Central Pacific would start in Sacramento, California, and build east.

stations. People who saw the signs would want to buy a paper to read all about it.

At the first train station, Tom sold thirty-five papers. (Most days he sold only two or three there!) That gave him a brand-new idea: If people really wanted the news, they might pay more than usual to get it. Tom raised the price of the paper at the next station. And he raised it again later. Still people bought his newspapers.

Tom was creative and could guess how people might react to his new ideas. Before too long those qualities would make him a famous inventor.

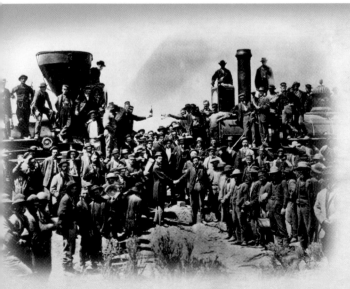

◀ THE TWO RAILROADS met in Promontory, Utah.

The U.S. government chose the place where the tracks would meet— Promontory, Utah.

On May 10, 1869, the rails were joined. Two locomotives stood facing each other. Four special spikes connected the two sets of tracks. Railroad officials tapped the head of the last spike with a hammer. A nearby telegraph tapped out the word *done*.

That message raced across the nation. Finally people in the United States could travel by train from coast to coast.

T. A. EDISON.
Electric-Lights.
No. 214,636. Patented April 22, 1879.

...ated Mar. 1, 1887.

CHAPTER 4

The Young

INVENTOR

By the end of 1862, fifteen-year-old Tom was spending most of his time learning to be a telegrapher. Telegraphers had to use Morse code to translate coded messages quickly. Finally Tom became a "tramp telegrapher." That means he worked for a few weeks or months at one place. Then he moved on to another.

◄ TOM THE TELEGRAPHER
preferred to work at night.

Tom liked working the night shifts best. That left him time to read during the day. He could also work on his experiments and tinker with inventions. But Tom had trouble holding some of his jobs. One time two trains nearly crashed because Tom fell asleep! (He was supposed to send a signal when the oncoming train came through.) Tom lost that job, but he soon got another. With practice he became a very fast telegrapher.

An Unpopular Invention

In 1868 Tom got a job in Boston, Massachusetts, with Western Union—the company that owned the telegraph lines that sent messages across the country. He also got his first patent for an invention that year. Usually the first person to come up with an invention is the one who gets the patent. The inventor sends a drawing and a description of the invention to the U.S. government. The person who gets the patent for an invention is the only one who can make that item.

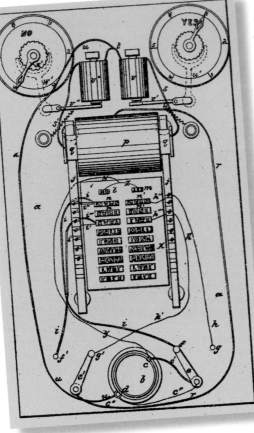

◀ DRAWING of the vote counter that Tom submitted to the U.S. Patent Office

During his life, Tom would get more than one thousand patents! His first was for an automatic vote counter. Tom thought the U.S. Congress would want to use it. When members of Congress vote on a bill, they have to keep track of how each person votes. Tom's counter would have done that. But officials liked counting votes by hand. So no one wanted to buy his invention. (Tom was ahead of his time: Today Congress uses machines to vote.)

The vote counter didn't make Tom any money. But he believed that even an idea that didn't work out was still a good thing. When Tom wanted to solve a problem, he just kept trying. He believed making mistakes would bring him closer to his goal. A few years later, he would show the world that he was right.

"Imagination Factory"

Tom left Western Union the next year and moved to New York City. He got a job with a company that made telegraph equipment. While Tom was there, he made his first successful invention. It was a machine that kept track of changing stock prices. Tom's *stock ticker* was not a brand-new idea, but it was a better model of a machine already in use.

Tom didn't stop there. He came up with new and better stock tickers. A company liked one of his machines so much, they wanted to own the right to build it. So they paid Tom $40,000 for it. (Getting $40,000 in 1870 was like getting $500,000 today!)

▶ **TOM'S STOCK TICKER** made it easier to track stock prices.

◀ **TOM'S EMPLOYEES** were treated with respect in his lab.

Tom had enough money to set up his own workshop. It was a place for people to use their imagination and their skills.

Everyone pitched in to get a job done.

Tom was an unusual boss. He didn't dress very neatly. He was not very strict and he liked to play jokes on the people he worked with. But Tom was a hard worker and he expected others to work hard, too. Tom also found he could get by with only a few hours of sleep at night if he took short naps during the day. He could fall asleep anywhere. He might sleep under a lab table or behind a door. After a nap Tom would go right back to work.

One of Tom's workers was a girl named Mary Stilwell. Tom and Mary fell in love and were married in December 1871. The couple had three children—Marion, Thomas Jr., and William. Tom's nicknames for two of the children came from Morse code. He called

▶ **MARY STILLWELL** worked for Tom when she was sixteen. She married Tom in 1871.

Marion "Dot" and little Thomas "Dash."

In 1876 Tom moved the family and the business to Menlo Park, New Jersey. Soon the eyes of the world would be on Menlo Park and the amazing work Tom was doing there.

Fast FACTS

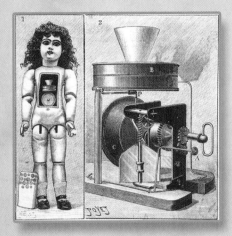

Here are a few of Edison's many inventions:

- The first socket to hold a lightbulb

- A meter to measure how much electricity a house uses

- A talking doll (It had a tiny phonograph in it.)

- An electric pen that was used to make more than one copy of a document at a time

- A way to send four telegraph messages over one wire at once

- A way to vacuum-pack foods so they stay fresh longer

CHAPTER 5

Sound

WRITING

For Tom 1877 was a very big year. He was working on many projects at once. The year before, Alexander Graham Bell had invented and patented the first telephone. But it did not work very well. Tom came up with a way to make it work much better.

He was also working on new parts for the telegraph. One day Tom had a lucky "accident." He found a way to record the sound of the human voice! For his first recording, Tom spoke some of the words to "Mary Had a Little Lamb."

◀ BELL'S early telephone looked like this.

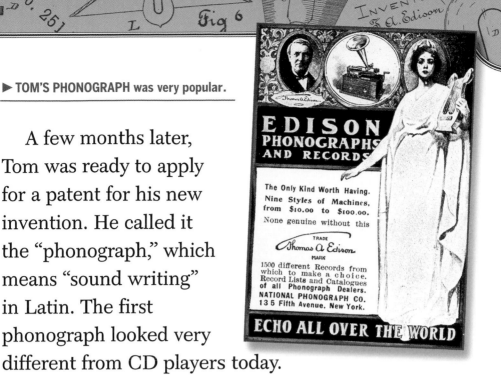

▶ TOM'S PHONOGRAPH was very popular.

EDISON
PHONOGRAPHS
AND RECORDS

The Only Kind Worth Having.
Nine Styles of Machines,
from $10.00 to $100.00.
None genuine without this

TRADE
Thomas A. Edison
MARK

1500 different Records from
which to make a choice.
Record Lists and Catalogues
of all Phonograph Dealers.
NATIONAL PHONOGRAPH CO.
135 Fifth Avenue, New York.

ECHO ALL OVER THE WORLD

A few months later, Tom was ready to apply for a patent for his new invention. He called it the "phonograph," which means "sound writing" in Latin. The first phonograph looked very different from CD players today. Instead of a flat disk, it used a cylinder—a shape like a paper towel roll. A thin sheet of foil was wrapped around the cylinder. Sounds were recorded on the foil and could be played back.

People were amazed by the phonograph. Tom was invited

▲ THE FIRST PHONOGRAPH
Tom listens to the sounds from his invention.

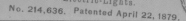

CHAPTER 6

Another
BRIGHT IDEA

The bright idea behind the lightbulb was simple. A piece of metal or carbon (called a *filament*) was hooked up to two wires. Electricity passed through the filament. As it heated up, it began to give off light. But no one could solve one big problem: As soon as it began to glow, the filament would always burn up. And that was the end of the light.

> "I have not failed. I've just found 10,000 ways that won't work."
>
> —THOMAS EDISON

Tom had to find a material that would glow for a long time. In October 1878 he told the press that it would take him just six weeks.

However, it would take more than a year. During that time, Tom and his workers tried one filament after another. They tried many types of paper and many kinds of wood. They tried linen, grass, and tar. They even tried horsehair and human hair. Each time the bulb burned out too fast, but Tom never got discouraged. He just made a note of the result and started over again.

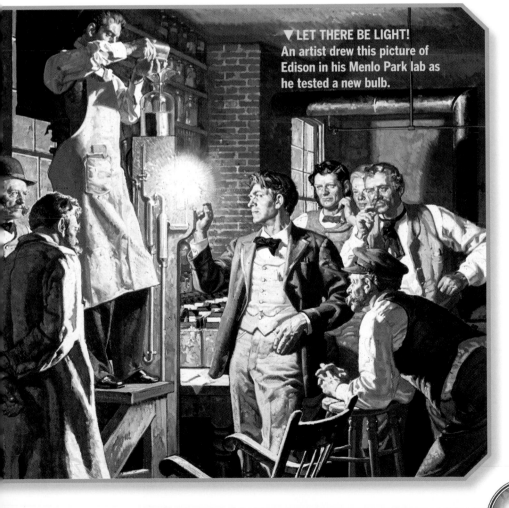

▼ LET THERE BE LIGHT!
An artist drew this picture of Edison in his Menlo Park lab as he tested a new bulb.

Let There Be
LIGHT
(Bulbs)!

You won't find a baked-cotton wire inside today's lightbulbs. Instead, there is a small wire that is made of the metal tungsten. This wire is called the filament. When electricity flows through the wire, it heats up and glows. The filament gives off light. There is very little air inside the bulb. This keeps the filament from burning up right away.

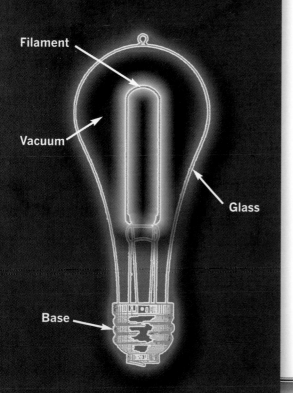

Filament

Vacuum

Glass

Base

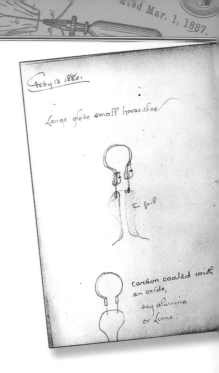

Feby 13 1880.

Large globe small horseshoe

Tin foil

carbon coated with an oxide, say alumina or lime.

▲ TOM MADE these drawings of a bulb.

Finally, in October 1879, he tried a piece of cotton thread that had been baked in an oven first. It glowed for thirteen hours! Tom knew that he had done it. And he proved it to the world when all of Menlo Park, New Jersey, glowed in electric light on that cold New Year's Eve in 1879.

Tom was thrilled, but he still had work to do.

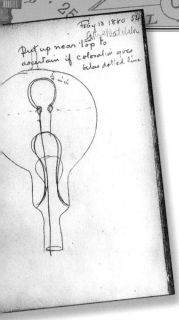

He wanted the bulb to glow even longer. And that was just the beginning. After all, there were no lamps to put the bulbs into. There were no switches to turn the lights on. There was no wiring in people's homes. There was no electric company supplying the power.

A lightbulb was useless without all the things needed to make it work. Tom went back to the lab and invented them all.

▲ EDISON NEVER GAVE UP. He kept trying until he got his inventions to work.

T. A. EDISON.
Electric-Lights.
No. 214,636. Patented April 22, 1879.

...nted Mar. 1, 1887.

Fig. 2.

CHAPTER 7

The GREAT MAN

After Thomas Edison created his lightbulb, he was a great hero—both in the United States and all over the world.

He was only thirty-two when he showed off the first practical bulb, but he had the respect of many experienced (and wealthy) business people. He could get people to invest money in his ideas.

▶ **THOMAS ALVA EDISON became a successful and rich businessman.**

When they found out that Thomas Edison was involved in a project, they became excited. They believed he could do anything.

But life wasn't always happy for Tom. In 1884 his wife, Mary, became very sick. When she died in August, Tom was deeply sad. He spent a lot of time with his daughter, Dottie. And he kept busy because he thought that hard work would stop him from feeling too sad.

Life with Mina

In 1885 he met a young woman named Mina Miller. Mina was well educated, and her family was wealthy. Her father was an inventor, too. After a few months, Tom wanted to ask Mina to marry him.

▲ TOM AND HIS SECOND WIFE, MINA, were married for forty-five years.

He proposed to her in a very unusual way. Tom used Morse code to tap out his question in Mina's hand. She happily tapped her answer back: Dash, dot, dash, dash. Dot. Dot, dot, dot. (That's the word *yes* in Morse code.)

Tom and Mina were married in New Jersey

▲ TOM'S LAB in West Orange, New Jersey, had the latest equipment.

on February 24, 1886. They moved into a large house called Glenmont in West Orange, New Jersey. Tom built a huge new lab nearby. It was ten times bigger than his lab at Menlo Park! For Tom, it was like a giant playground. At his new lab he could tinker and invent as much as he liked.

Tom and Mina had three children together—Madeleine, Charles, and Theodore. Tom loved his wife and children very much, but he spent most of his time working. His business trips were hard on his family because they missed him.

The Motion Picture Business

Telegraph messages. Telephones. Recorded music. Electric light. Daily life was changing fast. People had come to expect wonderful new inventions every few years. What would be the next amazing creation? How about moving pictures?

Edison's lab came up with a machine called a "kinetoscope." It did not show movies on a big screen. Imagine watching a small TV through a pair of binoculars. A simple silent movie that Tom made was loaded into the machine. One person at a time could look at the movie. The

TOP 5
Inventions

Could you live without a lightbulb? In a magazine poll, one thousand people ranked the most important modern inventions. Are these your Top 5, too?

AUTOMOBILE 63%

LIGHTBULB 54%

TELEPHONE 42%

TELEVISION 22%

ASPIRIN 19%

viewer had to turn a handle to make the film move.

People were very excited. They had never seen motion pictures before. Moving pictures were a new kind of entertainment. Now there was a need for movies to show in the machine. So Tom built a movie studio in West Orange. It was the first movie studio ever! He also helped invent a camera for filming motion pictures. Tom and his staff became moviemakers. Their films were short—some were only sixteen seconds long! The films didn't really have stories. One showed boxing matches. Another showed Edison working in his lab, and a third showed people dancing.

Other inventors

◀ TOM'S COMPANY
began making movies
using their cameras.

came up with the kind of moving pictures that we see

today. Before long they replaced Tom's moving pictures. Eventually, they had sound as well as pictures. But without Tom and his staff, "movies" would not have come along as fast as they did.

▶ LIGHTS, CAMERA, ACTION!
Edison shows off his motion picture camera. Compare it with a modern camera.

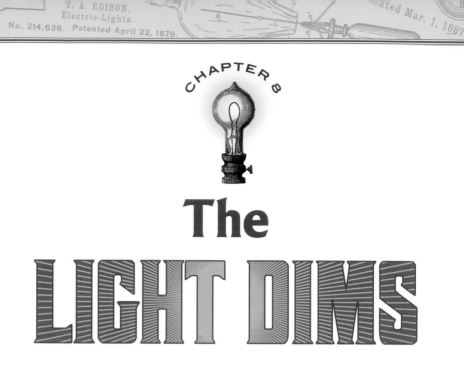

CHAPTER 8

The
LIGHT DIMS

By the end of the nineteenth century, Thomas Edison was a rich man. He could have stopped working any time he wanted. But he *never* wanted to stop working! He continued to make improvements in phonograph records. He worked for years on creating a battery that could store a lot of power. He even tried using cement as a building material for homes!

Helping the War Effort

In 1917 the United States entered World War I. The government asked Tom to lead a group of scientists and inventors to work on ideas to help win the war.

► EDISON'S INVENTIONS,
including a device to locate enemy
planes, helped win World War I.

Tom's team thought of ways to protect ships from torpedoes. They came up with ways to locate enemy airplanes and submarines. Tom also figured out how to make many chemicals that were needed during the war. He set up factories to make the chemicals that were in short supply.

The war ended in 1918. In the years that followed, Tom spent a lot of time working on the phonograph and developing records. Even when he began to feel weak and sick, he kept working. He believed in hard work. He said it made him live longer.

◄ HARD WORK kept Edison going.

In 1928 Thomas Edison was given a Congressional Gold Medal—one of the nation's highest civilian awards. It was for all the amazing work of his lifetime. The leaders—and the citizens—of the United States wanted to thank him for making their lives better and easier. They wanted to thank him for bringing honor to America.

Thomas Edison died on October 18, 1931. He was eighty-four years old. Three days later

▶ LONGTIME FRIENDS
Edison was friends with Henry Ford, who made automobiles. These two sucessful businessmen and inventors changed our lives.

Museums of a GENIUS

electric lights all over the United States were dimmed for one minute. It was a way of honoring the man who had lit up the world.

Thomas Edison will be remembered for his inventions and his belief that almost everything is possible. Work hard, ask lots of questions, never give up trying out your ideas, and treat people with respect. That's how Edison lived his life and reached his goals. There is a lesson in Edison's life for all of us.

The lab at West Orange (photo above) operated for some years following Edison's death. Today it is a National Historic Site, run by the National Park Service. Visitors can see the original labs. Many look the way they did when Edison worked there. (To check it out, go to www.us-parks.com.)

Glenmont, Thomas Edison's house, is now a historic site. Visitors can learn about the life of Edison and his family and see his furniture, artwork, and even Edison's cars.

T. A. EDISON.
Electric-Lights.
No. 214,636. Patented April 22, 1879.

ated Mar. 1, 1887.

Talking About
THOMAS EDISON

▲ Jim Quinn

TIME FOR KIDS editor Kathryn Hoffman Satterfield spoke with Jim Quinn about Thomas Edison. Quinn is the writer-in-residence at the National Inventors Hall of Fame in Akron, Ohio.

Q: *How many inventions did Edison patent?*
A: Edison patented 1,093 inventions, including some of the most important in history. That's still the world record.

Q: *What qualities did Edison have that made him a good inventor?*
A: Edison wouldn't let setbacks discourage him. He was so hearing impaired that people had to shout to talk

◀ THE LIGHT MAGICIAN is a sculpture in France made of lightbulbs.

to him. It made him sad that his deafness isolated him from others. But he figured that being deaf made it easier for him to concentrate on work. He even said he wouldn't have been such a great inventor if he had been able to hear normally.

Q: *How have some of his early inventions been changed or improved upon for use today?*
A: Today's lamps are brighter, cheaper, and last longer than the originals. Today's movies look and sound much better than the ones Edison made. His early recordings were hard to hear and wore out quickly. Today's CDs sound great and last a long time.

Q: *What can we learn from Edison?*
A: Success doesn't come immediately. Work hard and don't quit.

▶ RECORDINGS are smaller and longer lasting than ever before.

Thomas Edison's
KEY DATES

1847 — Born on February 11 in Milan, Ohio

1863 — Takes a job as a telegraph operator

1876 — Moves his business to Menlo Park, New Jersey

1877 — Develops the phonograph and records the human voice

1879 — Invents first practical lightbulb

1886 — Marries Mina Miller after death of his first wife

1894 — Opens the first motion-picture studio

1928 — Receives the Congressional Gold Medal

1931 — Dies on October 18; buried at Glenmont in West Orange, New Jersey

1861 Abraham Lincoln becomes the sixteenth president of the United States.

1913 Oreo cookies are introduced to cookie lovers.

1929 The U.S. stock market crashes.

UNEMPLOYED BUY APPLES 5 EACH